INTRODUCTION

Golf is one of those games t
massive high once you feel
struck right out of the middle of the golf club. That
sweet sound and feel is a haven of pleasure in your
hands and arms. The one shot that's worth waiting
for. The envy of all your golfing partners.

On the other hand, we have all experienced the bad
shots. The shots that make us think 'how did that
happen'? Leaving us in a quandary trying to figure out
whether it was the head lifting up or the grip was in a
poor position from the start and got worse as though
there's some special oil placed on the handle of the
club purposefully to ensure we hit one of the worst
shots of our golfing career.

It's not the lack of good/perfect shots that hurt our
games, it's the (very) bad shots that creep in every
now and again. The ones that are struck on a
previously unused part of the clubface. The ones that
go in a direction that's completely alien to the player.
The ones that you feel are so simple that even
beginners can make but yet still manage to screw up.
The ones that you feel you've made exactly the same
swing as you have done all day, but the ball
disappears into a different direction never to be seen
again. It's these shots that do the harm and it's these
shots that need to be eradicated from people's
games if progress is meant to be made and potentials
reached.

Jack Nicklaus famously said once that he hit not more than 2 perfect shots in every round of golf that he played. 2!!! This is the most successful golfer on the planet, winning 18 major tournaments in the process and he only hit 2 (in his words) perfect shots per round! How did he win all those titles and all that money? His mistakes were better than everybody else's. Whilst everyone else was making bogey, he made par. His bad shots were better than everybody else's.

It's not all about hitting the perfect shot...... far from it. It's about making sure your misses, your bad shots, are better than your bad shots of the past.

You obviously want to improve your golf otherwise you wouldn't have taken the plunge and purchased this book. So I am going to keep things very simple and concise to help and enable you to achieve what you would like in this game and draw on my experience I have had over the past 15 years of coaching the game to over 10,000 individuals.

If you're wanting a golf book full of technical information or golf from a scientific perspective, sorry, this isn't for you. This is for the club golfer who simply wants to get better. After all, the average handicap of a club golfer (16) has not decreased in over 50 years!!! Why is that, after the introduction of new technology, better golf balls and huge clubheads the size of a Wok, the tools we use to play golf have improved immensely, so why hasn't the average handicap decreased? Simply put, golfers haven't improved and have made the game more complicated than it should be.

This book is all about simplicity, understanding why bad shots happen and, more importantly, understanding what you can do to improve. Call it a 'hit list' if you were of myths uncovered and stories of my years of teaching all types of player, from young to old, to elite to beginner.

Everyone's journey in the game of golf is unique. Everyone hits the ball differently from the next person along the line on the driving range but it's all about reaching your potential. How far you can go in the game and what level can you reach, that's the exciting part. Not 'can I be the next Rory McIlroy' it should be 'can I beat my score from last week'.

When I took up golf at the age of 6 it enthralled me. How does this little white ball fly this far and why can I not do it all the time! It really was a puzzler to me and it's all I ever wanted to do. Play on the major tours, travelling the world playing the game that I had a huge amount of passion for due to it's unique nature and surroundings. However, it didn't work out like that and I never fulfilled my potential with what I thought at the time was a lot of effort and energy that I put into the game which left me asking 'why'? Why did I put in so many hours of play and practice just to miss a lot of cuts and shoot high scores? Why did I love practice but dislike first tee nerves in a competition? Why did I end up feeling fearful on a competitive round of golf and why did I play my best with my mates in a social encounter? These questions led me to where I am today. After years of research into finding answers for these questions and many more (remember, learning never stops, no matter how old or experienced you are), it has helped me help others enjoy and improve their golf games that little bit more. And that's where I get my adrenaline from, helping me pass on the answers to the mistakes I made as a golfer and ensuring that no-one else falls out of love with the game to the degree that I did. Let's be honest, golf is a tough game and it makes it worse if we know we can perform to a good level but one or two bad days has a negative effect on a lot of players and enthusiasm wanes. It's my duty as a golf coach to ensure this enthusiasm remains to all who play the game.

Everyone is unique and different. Some people are tall, some small. Some are wide, some are narrow. Some are powerful, some are weaker. Some love to analyse, others like simple. Some like to question, others like to listen.

This is why I love teaching the game. Having played, fairly unsuccessfully, I wanted to find out what I did wrong and why I wasn't successful. I used to dream as a child of winning the Open or playing in the Ryder Cup (the closest I got to playing the Ryder Cup was playing in alternative called 'The Cyder Cup') but never achieved those dreams and, at the time, I didn't know why. Curiosity got the best of me and I wanted to find answers. Answers that could help me discover why I wasn't able to achieve the status of 'best golfer in the world' and answers, more importantly, that could help others achieve what they wanted to in the game. This search led me to hundreds of books, DVD'S, trips to see numerous coaches and many, many seminars on all things that improves the games of others.

This book is aimed towards any golfer who has fought against the so called 'demons' in their body or mind, who have played the game for years without achieving what they wanted to achieve from the game.

It's aimed at anyone who wants to take up the game. What to expect, what to look out for and what to savour in all that's good in the game.

Read it as you want. Skip through it. Browse. Read it from back to front. But most of all, enjoy it and be entertained by it. After all, golf is a game of entertainment.

And if you get one thing out of it that will help you cut your handicap, play better golf, or generally just have a better time playing, I can safely say I'll be a happy coach.

Dedicated to my Mom and Dad. Inspirations.

Two in a million.

'I can do it on the range, but can't on the course'

I hear this a lot, mainly from low handicappers but all club golfers tend to be prone to this 'disease'. The ability to swing with pure freedom and ease on the driving range, a mountain of pristine golf balls just waiting to be dispensed from the bucket and struck down an area of vast grassland and no hazards whatsoever bring very little consequence to the shot. We can hit the worst shot possible, but the worst thing that can happen to us is the embarrassment of a poor shot if someone on the range is watching.

There is no real consequence to our shots on the range. We won't get punished a shot if it goes out of bounds, we won't lose our shiny new Callaway ball in the water on the range, we won't look like a fool if we're searching through endless rough and strike a tree on what feels like every hole on the range. There just isn't the same atmosphere and mindset on the range that's needed for the golf course due to the fact there is simply a lot less pressure on the range than compared with out on the golf course, far less consequences.

For all you hard-core practisers out there (come on, admit it!) who go the range or practise area everyday......... I salute you! Although you need to improve your routine if you are prone to this very common disease of super range play but not demonstrating this on course.

I told this story to a 14 handicapper. Good player, but couldn't quite get down to that elusive single figure handicap he'd been working towards his almost 20 years of playing the game. It wasn't his technique that was the issue....... It wasn't his short game that was the issue...... it was how he practised that was the issue. He just aimlessly hit balls, not even picking a target on the range to aim at. He was purely practising his swing, not practising Golf.

Now some of you will say that's fine and I agree, sometimes you must work on your swing on the range, especially when you're working on changes with your coach. But, when your technique is good (and this guys was) you need to start thinking of the shot rather than the swing. MAKE YOUR PRACTISE TOUGHER THAN YOUR PLAY. Set challenges, pick targets, curve the ball, challenge your friends, make it hard and put yourself under pressure on the range. You'll have fun in doing so and, when it comes to the course, you will relish those tough shots over water or tight pins hugging the deep rough as you'll have practised the mindset you need for these on the range.

And the 14 handicapper? He got down to single figures within 8 months of practising better habits and thinking about the golf shot rather than his swing.

'Keep your head down'

It's a classic anecdote. We've all heard it. A favourite piece of advice from your playing partners, opponents, husband or even a stranger who sees you struggling on the driving range. They tell you you're hitting bad shots because you are not looking at the ball. A myth beyond all recognition!

You don't hit bad shots because you're not looking at the ball. I can tell you that without even seeing your swing.

How do I know this?

Take a look at former world number 1 David Duval.

He wasn't even looking at the ball at the point of impact and he was one of the best players of their generation. It certainly didn't harm him in achieving their goals in the game!

So why has this been such a popular phrase and why does it not help us?

It's a fairly obvious statement that we need to, at some stage in the swing, look at what we are striking. However, golfers go to the extreme of this at times, leaving the golfer unable to turn their shoulders because their chin is in the way, desperately trying to keep their head DOWN as this is what they have been advised.

We have been hardwired to think like this!

To distil the myth and put it into more useful content, we need to rephrase this most famous golf tip………..
We don't need to keep our head down, we need to keep our head more 'STABLE' Or 'CENTRED' over the ball. The head HAS to move slightly in the swing to accommodate all the motion that's necessary in making an efficient swing, but we do need to limit the motion……. Limiting the sway from side to side and limiting the movement up and down.

Next time you are offering advice to a friend or family member who is catching the top of the ball or catching the ground a lot and if you aren't a coach, tell them to simply brush the turf with the club, which leads nicely onto our next story………………………

Divots

I once had a gentleman for a lesson, in his 70's, who used to play off a 9 handicap but has crept up and up as he has matured in years to a 19 handicap. You can imagine he was a tad annoyed about creeping ever closer to the 20's seeing as he was a former single figure golfer, something only a small percentage of golfers ever achieve.

It was his first lesson and, before we started, I asked him, as I do with all golfers on their first lesson, what they want to get from their game and what have they been working on, if anything, this past few rounds or practise sessions.

This guy was very honest. He said he watches a lot of golf, especially the PGA Tour, with lush fairways and quick greens. He had noticed something very striking in all the time he'd been watching the best players in the world in action. He noticed they took HUGE divots! Even some taking divots with their fairway woods and hybrid clubs. Now, I bet you know what he was trying to do in his game? Yep, he tried to take as big a divot as the pros on the TV.

'But why is that a bad thing this guy tried to do that?' I hear you say. Well, first of all, here was a man who predominantly cut across the ball and hit slices, played on fairly soft courses, especially in the winter, and he was trying to hit DOWN on the ball to an extreme effect to emulate those tour professionals and take big divots to help, what he thought, enabled him to play better golf and reach that level he had before.

Unfortunately, the tactic was not working for him and he was getting frustrated with his game and, quite literally, was hacking up the course taking divots the size of a small country with the ball going barely 30 yards.

Our first session took place on the golf course on a rather damp day, the kind this player didn't like for obvious reasons. What did he do down the first hole? First 4 shots were heavy, huge great divots with him hitting very much down on the ball, attempting to copy the worlds best.

Now for me this was an easy one. No need for technical instruction, no need for mechanics or endless amounts of time needed to spend out on the practice area. I simply said to him, 'brush the turf, feel as though you're taking the top layer of grass off and hardly touching the soil underneath'. This idea was completely alien to him! 'Well hang on, why do the pros take big divots?' he asked me. I explained to him that because they generate lots of club speed and create a consistently good angle of attack (approx. 4 to 6 degrees down with a short iron) they are able to make that ball then turf contact. When (with all due respect to him) 70 plus year olds don't generate the same club speed and when they hit excessively down on the ball (approx. 8 to 10 degrees down) you get the turf ball contact that so many amateur golfers dread, watching the ball trickle 10 yards in front when they had 120 to go.

After 5 in a row that were the 5 sweetest shots he had struck in a long time, the penny dropped for him! It was like a miracle had occurred, a eureka moment as I like to describe it! He simply had to feel the club bruising the turf. He didn't have to take massive chunks out the ground to be able to play his best golf, he barely had to touch the turf to get the ball to where he wanted it to go.

The divot tells us a lot about your swing and how you play golf. Do you take a divot? Do you take too much of a divot? Next time you're out on the course, take a look and see how much turf, if any, you take up during your shot. A lot of people put emphasis and thought into the swing when the swing can't give us much feedback into why we played a good shot or a bad shot. On the other hand, a divot can tell us a hell of a lot and provide us with necessary feedback......... direction of swing and angle of attack (hit down too much = big divot, hit too much up = no divot).

Don't try and emulate the best in the world when it comes to divots or you will probably leave a lot of greenkeepers unhappy!

To Think or not to think? That is the question

How much is too much thinking when you get on the course? Do you think enough? Do you think too much? Do you not think at all when you get onto the course?

There's no doubt that there is a lot to think about in the game of golf. Golfers on the endless search for the perfect swing, trying to 'find' their putting stroke for the day, trying to get a sense of where the predicted ball flight of the round is to be, whether it be right to left or left to right.

I have had many many people say to me they go from one extreme to the other on the course....... From thinking too much to thinking very little. But how many swing thoughts are we allowed on the course at any one time?

The answer? One.

One swing thought. A thought about the feel around the green. A thought about the shot. A thought about what you want to do with the shot.

As long as it purely one thought. The human brain can only take one thought when trying to perform a task and, especially if it's something fast and complex like the golf swing, one thought is crucial.

Swing thoughts are often classed as a bad thing whilst on the course and, whereas I agree mostly to this statement, there is no harm in having one thought/feeling when trying to swing the club. It's when golfers have 2/3/4 swing thoughts per shot and, usually, very different swing thoughts around the course.

Think of it like this. Say I had 90 shots in a round of golf and I had 2 completely different thoughts per shot, that's 180 different elements that could be influencing our brain which sends out muscles into 'human mayhem'!

'Shall I tuck my elbow in?', 'Are my toes splayed out'?, 'Am I overswinging'?, 'Am I swinging too much from the inside'? These are just a few examples of swing thoughts that golfers can have and, unfortunately, can happen in just one swing.

You are far better off having one solid thought for the day. If you have lessons and, if the pro is worth his salt, he will give you no more than one thing to work on, concentrate on that. Don't concentrate on anything you hear on YouTube or have read about online............ the information might be completely irrelevant to what you need to do as a golfer to improve. We live in an age where there is copious amounts of information at our fingertips which is great, but our brains can only take so much information.

Focus on one swing thought..... AND ONE ONLY!

This leads us nicely onto…………

The 'Let's try this' syndrome

Come on, admit it, you have had tips from your mates who are decent golfers (14/15 handicap) been around the game for a while, you're not having the best of days, hitting the ball thin, hitting it heavy. What do your friends do? Offer advice to help you! Now, this is what is great about the game of golf, the sportsmanship, the camaraderie, the want to help other people we see who are struggling to get to grips with their game. Can you imagine this happening in football? Liverpool beating Manchester United 3 – 0 at half time and the Liverpool manager comes into the Manchester United dressing room to give the players advice on how they could play better! It would never happen!

However, treat this advice with caution. Most of the advice that golfers have to give is something that was mentioned to them but might not be correct for you. For example, player 1 is topping the ball a lot. There are numerous ways that the ball could be topped (swinging excessively over the top, head raising up, club excessively shallow, too much lag……… to name but a few). Player 2 listens to the advice (lifting head). Player 2 tries to do what player 1 has told him but it doesn't work. Player 2 becomes more frustrated. Player 1 says you aren't doing it right. Player 2 attempts to hit player 1 with 7 iron!!!!

Don't just go out onto the course and try the latest swing technique you have just heard or what your friends have told you. Test it on the range first. There is nothing that can go wrong on the range, there are a lot of things that can go wrong on the course.

The straight left arm (or not)

'The left arm has to be straight at the top of the backswing', says many a golfer! But the trouble is, many golfers can't explain why they think it has to be straight!

In fact, it's more detrimental if a golfer TRIES to keep the left arm straight (for a right handed golfer).

But why is this a myth and why do so many people believe it?

For starters, we need to understand how this myth came about and why.

Early instruction books were the instigators. The need to keep the club away from the body, creating width and, more importantly they said, creating power. Keeping the left arm straight (again, for a right handed golfer) actually diminishes the amount of power delivered to the golf ball and creates tension in the golf swing, where the necessary smaller muscles (wrists) needed to 'crack the whip' of the golf club are not able to do their job. A purposefully straight left arm can create shots such as a thin or a heavy contact, meaning the low point of the golf club (the bottom of the arc of the swing) is going to be inconsistent at best.

I can understand why old instruction books were very 'pro' straight left arm, but in my opinion the best way of creating power and the ability to more consistently strike the bottom of the ball and the ground at the correct position as often as possible is to ensure the club shaft is as far away from your shoulders at the top of the backswing. This will help create that width and necessary power needed to exchange into the transition of the downswing without adding to any tension in the upper body and arms in particular. TENSION IN THE SWING IS A KILLER!

Take a look at 2015 Masters champion Jordan Spieth, Robert Allenby and Calvin Peete to name but 3 elite players who have bent left arms at the top of their swing. They haven't done too badly for themselves in the game!

Junior Golfers (and parents)

There is no better sight than watching kids swing the club and rip the ball as far as they can. As adults, we stand back in astonishment to see 8 year olds sometimes hit it further than they do! The sheer effort, balance and poise is great to watch. But how do they do it? And, more importantly, how do they continue to do this towards their adult lives?

The trouble is with a lot of parents they tend to live their dream of being a Tournament professional with their child (not being sexist, but it's predominantly fathers who are guilty of this) and therefore put a lot of pressure on their child to perform, offering advice on every single shot they hit, whether it be on the course or on the range. The prospect of their sibling being the world number 1 golfer is a delight in their mind and they can see the pound signs in front of them when they turn their kids into human cash machines that tournament golf brings.

However, what parents sometimes don't realise is that with this attitude they are doing more harm than good to the child. Children make mistakes. Adults make mistakes. We learn from these mistakes by participating and doing. The trouble stems from parents who see mistakes (in golfing terms 'bad shots') as not good, as though they should be hitting perfect shots all the time. Perfect performance never happens in sport, let alone golf. Children just want to hit the ball as hard and as far as possible. Let them do that and ONLY offer advice if they ask. Never ever ever get behind the child and manipulate them into what you perceive as better positions in the set up and swing. You're doing more harm than good. Let them enjoy the game, let them love the game and the rest will take care of itself, whether they go onto being a Tournament professional, a teaching professional, a club golfer or just an occasional player.

Just to give you a stat, the chances of your son/daughter being a world number one golfer? You have more chance of winning the lottery twice over!

The Grip

How do you grip the club? Overlap? Interlock? 10 finger (all 10 fingers on the club)? Strong left hand? Strong right hand? Weak left hand? Weak right hand?

There are a number of ways to grip the golf club but which is the correct way and which is the wrong way?

Now I'm going to give you an answer that you might not like as it's something that you will never have heard before and goes against the grain of what almost every instruction book has ever delivered to you............... it depends! In my experience I have seen players grip it 'text book' as per the standard instruction books and hit the ball left, right and with an incorrect wrist hinge. I have, on the other hand, seen some extra-ordinary hands on clubs that manage to do the job for that player. Don't get me wrong, I would advocate an orthodox grip on a player who has literally just started to play the game or has played just once or twice. If I was coaching a player who has played for 10 years for example and never had a lesson, the grip is something I would try and avoid if possible changing. Why? Because a player who has been playing for that length of time would find it very difficult to change the position of their hands as they are very used to the feeling of where their hands are positioned on the club, it's unconscious and they've found a way to match their swing to their grip. The difficulty comes when changing the hands, the only point of contact with the golf club, becomes conscious and thus the player ends up 'fighting' in the short term to get a comfortable feeling on the grip, whether it be the correct way or not, leading to a steering of the clubface opening or closing it with the ball ending up left or right of target.

I remember teaching a gent who had the most un-orthodox grip I've ever seen. He was a right handed player and his left hand was as strong as possible (meaning positioned 'on top' of the handle and able to see all of the back of the left hand during set up) and his right hand was also strong (meaning right hand 'under' the grip, so if palm of the hand were to open, it would point to the sky). Now, usually when I see a grip like this, the instant reaction is to see the ball flying left as the clubface would close. However, the player told me on his first session his bad shot was to the right of target! Completely against the grain of what his grip was saying! I was fascinated to see how his clubface was looking during the swing and especially at the moment of truth, impact. As expected, the clubface at the top of the swing was closed (clubface pointing at the sky at the top). But his clubface returned to impact as near to square as possible almost every single shot, the ball starting on line or a touch to the right consistently.

Curious, I wanted to do a little experiment with the golfer. I asked him to put his hands in an orthodox position……. Able to see 3 knuckles on left hand and thumb on right hand pointing to right shoulder. Instantly, he hated it. Having played for 6 years with his very strongly positioned grip, he took an instant dislike to it. I tried to comfort him by giving him a John Jacobs quote….'don't worry where the ball goes, I'll take the blame'.

Well, the next 3 shots he hit went so far right of target with a 6 iron it was incredible, even missing the 80 yard wide driving range! That was enough evidence for me, I wasn't going to let him carry on hitting shots like that. He came to me to improve, not miss the driving range every time he hit a shot!

My point here is don't try and make the grip perfect. It doesn't need to be spot on to help you hit quality golf shots. It might need tinkering here and there and for that go and see a reputable professional to help you. Other than that, unless you are a beginner, don't try and change your grip because a magazine article says so!

<u>Tee Up?</u>

The great part about what I do is that golfers ask questions..... lots of them! I love questions because if you don't ask questions, you don't get answers, and if you don't get answers, you don't improve at what you do!

A popular question I get asked is 'how high do I tee the ball up for a driver?'

With a question like this there are a few answers which I will come on to. As a rule of thumb however, I don't think you can go wrong with teeing the ball up so that HALF THE BALL IS ABOVE THE CROWN (TOP) OF THE CLUBHEAD. This is a sure-fire way of teeing the ball up a consistent height.

There are some potential elements where teeing up like this could be detrimental to you!

Firstly, as i'll explain in the next segment, the height of the tee should also be determined by THE ANGLE YOUR CLUB COMES INTO THE GOLF BALL. For example, if you hit 'down' on the ball, a low tee would suffice. If you attack the ball by hitting 'up' then a higher tee would be more to your advantage.

But I can hear you say now…..'How do we know what angle of attack I am?'…………

Angle of attack

When I ask children I teach at Whittlebury Park and at local schools what they think Angle of Attack means, they come out with some classics. 'How to attack your opponent' was one response. 'Is it something to do with fishing' was another.

I don't expect kids new to the game to understand what angle of attack is but I believe it's very important that experienced golfers wanting to improve understand the concept and importance of this. Get it right and it will help you strike the ball as well as you can and as efficiently as you can. Get it wrong and you could be hitting your driver the same distance as your 6 iron.

But what does it mean?

The angle of attack (or angle of approach it has been known as) is the vertical angle of the clubhead compared to the ground. Get the angle of attack wrong and you could be hitting fat or thin irons, with the driver you could be topping or 'skying' (popping up) the driver. All destructive shots and all very common mistakes in amateur golfers, sometimes occurring in professionals, albeit very rarely.

But what is the correct angle of attack and how do I achieve it?

This depends on what club you're hitting. For an iron, the club needs to hit downwards to 'pinch and collect' the ball from the surface (only slightly.........3 degrees down being a good number) with the driver ideally requiring an upward angle of attack due to the fact it is sitting up on a tee and has the 2nd lowest loft of any club in the bag (behind the putter). An upward angle of attack with a driver will help you launch the ball higher and lower the spin rate, leading to longer drives. For example, a player who swings the driver at 75 mph and hits down by 5 degrees can achieve a driver potential distance of 178 yards. A player who swings the driver at the same speed but hits UP by 5 degrees can achieve a potential distance of 199 yards due to higher launch and less spin being imparted on the golf ball.

I see too many higher handicappers hit down with the driver, usually resulting in the 3 wood or even some irons going further than the driver and questioning the need to use a driver.

The most effective way of hitting up on the driver and hitting down on a driver lies in the set up. For the driver, to hit more up on the ball, tilting the spine AWAY from the target (giving the impression and feel the right shoulder is lower than the left for a right-handed golfer). This will help the club move in more of an upward direction, enabling the low point of the golf club to be slightly before striking the golf ball, then the club has no choice to move upwards.

For the iron, to be able to hit downwards, is the opposite. The trick is to lean SLIGHTLY (I emphasise the word 'slightly') towards the target, with the handle of the golf club ahead of the ball at impact.

Take your medicine

Do you turn a bogey into a double or triple bogey? We obviously don't do these things on purpose but sometimes we just can't help it. Let's picture the scene. Easiest hole on the golf course, our anticipation on the tee is high as we are just about to encounter the most simple hole. A shortish par 4 with hardly any hazards apart from a couple of trees, a couple of low lipped greenside bunkers and some deep rough that doesn't come into play. Our mind races with thoughts of birdie or par at worse as we step onto the hallowed turf of the beginning of the hole. Driver off the tee……. Touch right but in play. Approach from 95 yards……. Slightly heavy, lands 10 yards short of the green in the bunker. Anger starts to creep in as we feel that was a simple shot to execute. Bunker shot from 18 yards………thin through the green! Chip back………. 25 feet from the hole. Steam is now driving through our ears as our anger is almost unmanageable. Letting the anger take over, we drive our first putt 5 feet past and miss the return, adding up to a 7 on the easiest hole!

Be honest, who's experienced this? I know I have. The sheer anger you feel when a hole we perceive as so simple, with no obvious danger on it and our expectations were high to begin with in the anticipation the simple hole should yield no worse than a par 4. However, with the inset of a poor second leading to the catalogue of errors, our negative mindset got the best of us and strategy went out of the window.

There are ways to avoid this scenario but, with the nature of the game of golf, can always show it's ugly face once or twice. Our goal is to make it happen less.

So how do we make it happen less? It's about managing our expectations. As we saw on the tee, the player had high expectations on the tee. The thoughts of the result (score) were stored in the mind even before the ball was placed on the tee. Never get up to a hole expecting to make a certain score. The only element we have influence over is the next shot we hit. Not the shot before, not in three shots time. The present shot should be the one we focus on. The process of that shot. After we strike, the outcome is generally out of our control. For example, a bad bounce when it lands. We have to accept that outcome and do our best on the process of the next shot. Many a scorecard has been ruined by golfers trying to place too much thought and emphasis on a results (score) based outcome

No such word as 'can't'

'I can't make the change'. 'I can't hole a putt for love nor money'. 'I can't hit the ball like I used to'. There are very good reasons for using the word 'can't' and the majority of them initiate from the brain!

Our brain rules our body. Whatever our brain tells our body to do, it usually does it. The problems come when our brain doesn't like something we've been asked to do. For example, grip changes are always difficult. If I thought a player had a weak grip which was causing the club face to open, I would try and manoeuvre the hands over to the right of the handle to make a stronger position, squaring or even closing the face slightly. However, our brain could reject the idea of changing the position of the hands. The brain can sense the hands have changed position and therefore we tell ourselves it's uncomfortable because it is out of the ordinary, we're out of our comfort zone as it's a feeling we're not used to. As a result, the hands and wrists stiffen and the brain rejects the idea of the new grip, forcing the hands back to their original position because the brain has said 'I can't get into this new position'!

I can bet your bottom dollar that if you stood up straight, let your arms hang down and I asked you to turn your hands to the right you could easily do it. So why doesn't the same happen when you're holding a golf club in your hands? It feels like we're squeezing the living daylights out of the club!

Purely because it feels out of the ordinary and we convince ourselves that this isn't right because it doesn't 'feel' right. It doesn't matter if you're paying £500 for a lesson with one of the worlds best instructors, we won't do it if we don't feel it's right. The only way to convince yourself is to hit balls and hit balls well. And then still even taking it onto the course we find tricky and keep saying to ourselves we can't do this because we want the safety net of comfort behind us which means going back to the old way of doing things and getting the same old results.

Tell yourself, in every walk of life, you CAN! Humans are amazing creatures at times if we talk to ourselves in the best way possible.

Golf's Greatest Invention

Video, bigger headed clubs, improved golf ball, launch monitors. The list goes on.

But what has been golfs greatest invention over the last 50 years?

Truth is there have been so many and everyone will have their own opinion with their own reasons for their choice.

In my opinion and my role as a coach, there has been nothing more influential than Trackman. Trackman has single handedly changed the ball flight laws by discovering and proving that the clubface has the biggest influence on the starting direction of the golf ball when, even in the recent past, it was thought the swing path was the biggest influencer of the balls starting direction.

If you haven't yet experienced Trackman, go seek a Professional who knows how to use one, what the numbers mean for you and can advise you on how to get better.

Bunkers

The elusive sand shot……… some courses have a lot of bunkers, some hardly have any at all, but if you can class yourself as a good bunker player then this will help your scores come shooting down. The confidence you will receive, even from just standing in the middle of the fairway, looking at a green surrounded by bunkers, and not be petrified of hitting the ball into one of those traps, is a massive step towards golfing greatness!

But what is the best way of getting out of them and, more importantly, hitting it close to the hole from even the deepest of bunkers?

Old coaching very much veered to the following set up to help the ball out of the bunkers:

- Open stance (for a right handed golfer feet aiming way left of target)

- Club head very open to target (pointing well right of target)
- Club path 'cutting across' golf ball (helped by the set up)

Now this was all very well and good but technology has helped players a lot in the last decade or so. When most players think about technology, we all think about the latest and greatest in driver technology to help us propel the ball as far as we could've possibly imagined. Yet wedge technology has gone relatively un-noticed. It's not classed as the 'sexy' part of the game. Technology in wedges has changed rapidly with wedge makers concentrating on the bounce of the club (defined as how much lower the trail edge of the sole is in relation to the leading edge measured in degrees) and the leading edge of the golf club which has become less sharp (more rounded) and the loft on the most lofted of wedges has increased with golfers using 64 degree wedges!

The need to really exaggerate the setup has gone. The loft and the bounce of the club does the work for us so there's no need to open the face up so much that it's pointing to the sky and therefore we don't need to aim as far left to the target. The big issue with the old way of setting up to a bunker shot was that we were so reliant of cutting across the ball it became more of a glancing blow rather than a full, meaty hit out of the centre. To envisage this, think about hammering a wooden stake into the ground. To get the full energy of the hammer into that stake, the hammer has to go up and down in a straight line. Now you imagine if the hammer was approaching the stake from a 45 degree angle side on........ how much energy is going into that stake now??? Not as much as there would be were the hammer to be travelling straight up and down on top of the stake.

To get the ball effortlessly off the clubface in the bunker and not thinning the ball through the green or leaving it in the bunker, we need to set up with a relatively square stance, opening up the clubface barely 2 degrees to give that ball just a touch more elevation. From there we simply try to strike a little bit of sand onto the grass bank in front of the bunker. The sand will then help elevate ball out of its position and, hopefully, end up close to the hole.

Goal setting

Whether you are a beginner or an experienced golfer, always go into a practice session, a lesson or on-course with a goal.

That goal should be a short-term goal, a goal that gives us satisfaction knowing it is achievable but difficult in a short space of time. Just one short term goal per round or practice session will soon add up to further long-term development.

Examples:

- Learn how to chip under pressure. Get 3 in a row within a club length of hole
- Hole 20 3-foot putts in a row to improve short putting
- Have 3 driving range sessions per week to give yourself time to work on one swing change

There are a ton of short term goals that can be reached, with all golfers requiring something different.

Bu the golden rule is to work on your weaknesses, don't just keep relying and practising your strengths. That will be in your comfort zone. We only improve and move forward by getting out of your comfort zone!

<u>With a little help from my friends!</u>

Do not take advice from friends or family members who either don't teach golf for a living or play off at least a scratch handicap! Do not do it. I repeat, do not do it! It leads to far more harm than good. The build up of what is usually false information that you don't need adding to thoughts in the brain that mix up the messages that need to be delivered to the muscles.

It's all well and good, especially when having a bad round of golf to take advice as your playing partners are the only ones that are seeing you swing. You trust them implicitly and take their advice on board like any good friend or family member naturally would. But don't do it! I have had to fix more swings than I've had hot dinners from players who have been given the wrong advice to help them fix their habits.

YouTube

This part follows the previous section in the way that all information which the golfer has self-discovered should be taken with a pinch of salt, in particular from anyone who has never seen you swing or from an untrained eye.

The introduction of YouTube in 2005 brought a whole new era to gaining information and enabling golf coaches to display their talents in improving golfers. Golfers worldwide can learn off the best. And best of all..........it's free! However, golf is an individual game. We are all physically different, we all have different stages of knowledge............ we are all individuals, so one person's way of getting rid of a slice might be completely different to another golfer's ability to eradicate the dreaded left to right curve ball.

So why do I pick on YouTube when it has so much good information out there?

Don't get me wrong, YouTube is a great tool and massively useful. As a coach, I can spend hours upon hours trawling through the countless videos of lessons and tips distributed to us by the world's best and most knowledgeable coaches. However, as an amateur golfer, I would avoid such videos. Why? Purely on the basis that they can add conscious thought into the mind that, more often than not, doesn't need to be there. Further information blocking the system.

For example, I remember teaching a gentleman. Good player, played to about 16-17 handicap so could hold his own around a course. Our first lesson was great, simple set up fix to get him striking the ball better and cleaner. He had a case of the heavy/fat shots when he came and when he left that was all but gone. (He was too crouched over the ball to begin with if you were wondering). All was well, he walked away happy and I was a happy coach knowing that he felt he was a better player because of how well he struck the ball. We ended the session booking the next one in 3 weeks later, to get used to the feelings and plan the way forward next for his golf.

3 weeks later, I was looking forward to seeing said player as I had the sneaky suspicion the results were going to be good on the basis he had changed something but got used to it straight away, a great confidence boost. A simple fix with instant results SHOULD mean a good, repeatable time on the course and range……. Or so I thought! I eagerly asked him

the question 'how have you got on this past few weeks'? expecting a positive reply. 'Terrible, worse I've ever played' came the reply. Shocked and gutted were the first two words to spring to mind from my perspective. Eager to find out what had happened, I questioned further. Was it a bad feeling about the set up? Was it swing mechanics broken down due to set up changes? Was it confidence in the new set up? None of the above................. 'I watched some videos on YouTube' came the reply. Now the penny had dropped. Because he was in search of perfection, he scanned the video sharing site for extra bites of information to help hit the flag everytime. It led to a lot of conscious thoughts in his mind that didn't need to be in there and, ultimately, led to worse results. All because he watched a few videos and tried to implement the changes they were recommending.

In golf, less is more. Less information over the most crucial areas of technique will help. Not feeding ourselves full of apparent words of wisdom that we feel will propel us to elite stardom in the matter of a few swings.

YouTube is great for a coach but not always great for a player. If you are to consume YouTube or any other swing analysis magazine out there on the market, I advise you watch the pros swing the golf club. Just watch over and over again. Don't try and copy positions they achieve in their swing, just watch a few times how they do it, their movement pattern, the impact area they get into. If this sort of imagery is available to you in your mind then that will be far more beneficial to you as opposed to endless theory about the biomechanics of the swing and splitting it into 30 different segments.

The FEAR of Golf

Fear……….. the dictionary definition being '*an unpleasant emotion caused by the threat of danger, pain, or harm*'

So why do so many people fear a bad shot or playing bad golf?
We aren't in danger if we play golf, unless we are in the firing line of a stray golf ball. We aren't in pain, unless we get hit by said golf ball. And we do ourselves no harm if we have a bad round of golf or hit a bad shot.

It's the emotional pain we go through. The near embarrassment we feel when we hit an 'abnormal' shot as we are the only ones to blame, we can't hide behind our team mates as golf is an individual sport. If we play Football, for example, and have one of the worst games of our life, nothing goes right, we have very few touches and contribute barely sweat to the team, it doesn't matter. We can easily hide behind the players that play well and our contribution barely goes unnoticed. Golf is very different. In Golf, if we have a bad round, especially when we play in a tournament with a scorecard in our back pocket, it appears like the whole world will find out how we've got on, especially in today's society of communicating through every nook and cranny. It's a dent on our ego, it's a strike on our pride, it hurts, especially when we know we can play so much better.

So how do we go about getting over this so called 'fear' that does not help us play the game to the best of our ability?

Firstly, we need to change our attitude. Going into a round thinking about all the things that can go wrong is one of the most fatal errors you can make. The probability of you playing your best with thoughts like that are slim to nothing. It can only go one way from there.

Now this is tough, because with golf, like no other sport, there are hazards............ lots of them! Trees, rough, water, bunkers, out of bounds to name but a few. There are indeed many things that can go wrong on a course. But what good is it to us if we ingrain these hazards into our mind before and during we play? Let me put it like this, if we consciously thought about avoiding all the hazards on a road when we're driving, we'd be a nervous wreck every time we got behind the wheel. We just drive, we don't worry that we desperately need to avoid hitting a parked car, we don't worry that an animal might run in front of us, we just do it and face the issues instinctively as opposed to constantly worrying about them.

We need to do the same on the golf course. We need to just let it happen and focus on what we DO want to do as opposed to what we DON'T want to do. The probability of us hitting better golf shots (or more importantly, better bad shots) increases dramatically.

<u>Knowing why you hit bad shots!</u>

I have had more than one golfer come to me with the problem of shanking! You know the shot, the swing feels great, perfectly normal, and then suddenly when we get to impact with the ball........ DINK, straight of the hosel/neck/heel (delete as appropriate) and we see the ball go straight right and very low.

The next shot, our minds a bit baffled with what just occurred, but we go again. Same swing, same nice feeling, then all of a sudden...... DINK, another one going low and to the right.
Right now, our anger levels and blood pressure are growing suddenly, we are hugely confused as the swing felt exactly the same as if we'd struck the ball out the centre of the golf club, but we ended up hitting one of 'those' shots, a shot that looks pretty ugly and can get us into a lot of trouble.

So what do we do to ensure it doesn't happen again?

Well, like most amateurs, we try and solve the issue by focusing on the swing. Trying to tinker with almost all of our limbs to get them into what we perceive as the perfect position to stop this from happening again. But what happens............ DINK! The changes

that we have made have not helped and our mind is now a blur of every single aspect of the swing that we have ever been taught, learnt or heard about. It's a disaster!
To avert this feeling, we need to ensure we KNOW why we have hit this shot. And by why I don't mean because X or Y have happened in the golf swing. I mean where has the ball made contact with the club!

In this case, the ball has hit the neck of the golf club, the part of the club where the shaft enters the head. BINGO! We have the answer, we know the ball reacts like that when it hits the hell and can also recognise the feel and sound that it makes when that occurs. All our task is next to ensure we strike the ball out of the opposite end of the golf club, the toe. And by this I don't mean trying to manipulate your body or think about the swing. I mean to simply try and strike the ball out of the toe.

Yes, different things will happen in the swing but the trick here is to not be conscious of these changes. Our task is to simply feel the ball coming out the toe anyway we can.
Results are everything in golf, it's not the one with the prettiest swing that shoots the lowest scores and wins tournaments.

Make sure the brakes stay off

Why is it when you're having a bad day on the course, the harder you try and fix it, the worse it gets?

We try and hit 'AT' the ball which often leads to impact position that's less than ideal.

Our brain, due to the fact we might hit some average or below average shots during the round of golf, wants to 'protect' what we have, in other words manipulate or try to control the club. Another way of this happening is by almost stopping the golf swing (putting the brakes on) just as soon as we've struck the ball to ensure we don't make our bad shots any worse.

Unfortunately, this is the single worst thing you can do if you're hitting bad golf shots. We need to allow the club to do it's work. If we purposely try and stop it then it won't work for us and the contact will be poor at best, more often than not coming out of the toe of the club and shooting off 45 degrees right of target (for a right handed player) and low.

We need to ensure we complete the swing, even if we're not having the best of days, even though you feel like fully swinging through will make it worse............ I will guarantee that it won't!

The Flight of the Ball Tells us All

As a coach, it is imperative that the student knows what is happening when a shot goes astray, and very few golfers (I'd estimate 5%) know why the ball flies in the direction that it does.

For example, the common misconception was if we were a right handed golfer trying to hook a ball around a tree in front of us (ball starting right of the tree and curving to the left), the general consensus was that the clubface needed to be closed (pointing left) at impact.

Below is a list of easy to understand rules on what the clubhead and face (path and face angle) must be doing at impact for the ball to react like it does. Please note that I am purely describing club characteristics and not swing characteristics. If we tried to hammer a nail into a piece of wood, would we be thinking about the movement of our hand and arm to nail it in or would we focus our attention on the hammer and nail (equipment). Have a look and think about your predominant ball flight and see what might cause those shots (all presuming right handed golfer). Note: this is assuming centred contact. The centredness of contact and will display a wide range of ball flights, depending on where the ball is struck. Also, assuming path numbers (degrees) are slightly greater than the face numbers (also measured in degrees):

CLUBFACE	OPEN (Right of target)	CLOSED (Left of target)
PATH		
In to Out (Swing Right)	Ball starts right and curves to target	Ball starts on target and curves left
Out to In (Swing Left)	Ball starts right and finishes further right	Ball starts left and curves to target

Note: If path and face were the same number and direction, the ball would not curve. E.g. Path 5 degrees right, face 5 degrees right

If it ain't broke, don't fix it

If you're shooting the scores of your life and feel as confident as you could possibly be, don't take a lesson! Only unless you're struggling with a certain area of your game, or indeed all of it, then take lessons. If a coach is worth his salt and you went to them to improve he wouldn't tell you anything, they would simply say keep on going. Don't let anything get in the way of a good streak!

Putting is an art, not a science

One of the big reasons I love this game is down to the fact that there are so many skills you need to help reach your golfing potential. Notice how I stay away from words like 'perfection' or 'master'……. These aren't achievable in the game.

From the power you need to hit your driver as far as you can to the feel and touch you need around the greens for chipping and putting, a whole range of attributes are needed to help you improve your golf game.

To ultimately lower your scores however, putting is crucial aspect. We will delve into putting a bit more during this book, but I wanted to start off with this point…………. Putting is all about feel, not about the science. What am I talking about?
Imagine you're rolling the ball underarm towards the hole from, say, 20 feet. What are you thinking about? Are you thinking about how you're holding the ball when you are about to roll it? Are you thinking about which point you have to release the ball from your hand? Are you thinking about how far back and through your arm has to travel in order to roll the ball closer to the hole? If you have answered yes to some or all of these questions you will not be a good putter.

Why???
Because the skill in putting is 'FEELING' your way instinctively to the hole. We all have that ability to roll the ball or throw an object towards something. For example, throwing a screwed up paper ball into a waste paper bin. Easy isn't it! Change of the position of the bin however or fire up the offices fans to create a lot of wind, it isn't easy. Why? Because we have included variables i.e. different positions and wind, our conscious mind takes over and tries to

control our throwing action. We therefore have less chance of throwing directly into the bin.

The same thought process applies to putting. As soon as you consciously focus on the action you are trying to perform, in this case the swing, the less chance you have of holing the putt on the basis you are not letting the body and therefore the putter do its work and what it needs to do. We are making variable compensations in our stroke meaning anything can happen, we can hit the putt long, short, left or right. If we focus purely on our target, like we do when we throw a paper ball in a waste paper bin, we let our natural instinct and movement to do its work and therefore give ourself more chance of hitting our target.

<u>It's not fair</u>

'Why am I 35 years old, the people who I usually play golf with are over 65 and they hit the ball 40 yards past me off the tee.........it's not fair'!!!

I hear this a lot. The younger, fitter golfer gets outdriven by their older counterpart who have never possessed biceps and are a foot smaller. How can this be?

For starters, it's a frustrating from the younger golfer's point of view. It wouldn't happen in any other sport! The older person would (rarely) beat a younger person in a 100m sprint. The younger person wouldn't be beaten (again, rarely) in a marathon. So why is it a regular occurrence that a supposedly stronger person can be many yards behind a comparatively weaker person when longer hitting takes a lot of strength?

It's all about the two 'T's………. Timing and Technique. The good news is that one comes with the other. If you have the technique, the body and the movement will find its natural sequencing motion, putting all the pieces of the puzzle in the right place, allowing the club to be at maximum speed and energy where it needs to be….. at impact.

However, if one person swings the driver at 90mph and another player swings the driver at 105mph per, who will hit the ball the furthest?

If you say the 105mph swinger will hit the ball further, you would be incorrect………on some level! Speed doesn't necessarily equal distance! Let me give you an example. If I was to hammer a large wooden stake into the ground, would I better off hammering at high speed/force hitting the stake from a horizontal angle or would I be better off striking the stake with the hammer with slightly less force/speed from a vertical angle? By far and away, you would be better off striking from the vertical angle at less force. Why? Purely on the basis the hammer when striking the stake would be 'on plane' in relation to the stake, compared to a very different angle if approaching the stake from horizontal. Try it. See how much energy is going into each hit from various angles.

So how does this help you hit the ball further than your playing partner who's 40 years your senior?

Check that your club is on plane. If it's not, it will sure eat up a lot of distance, no matter how hard you're trying to hit the ball.

<u>Sandy Lyle</u>

No, this is not a segment of the book dedicated to the great, major winning Scottish golfer. It's about bunkers and the association between 'Sandy' and bunkers (and also THAT shot from the 1987 Masters he hit to win the tournament).

In my experience you're either a very good and competent bunker player who can hit it close on most occasions or you struggle to hit the ball out of the bunker unless you thinned it 50 yards through the green. There seems to be a rather large dividing line between the two groups.

A lot of it, again, is down to confidence. But also a great deal is down to the technique and we all know confidence stems from good technique as mentioned earlier in the book.

So what makes a good bunker player? One of the best pieces of advice I ever got was from a superb coach by the name of Neil Plimmer. Neil specialises in junior golf and has invented the 'JOLF' brand of golf (Junior GOLF), enabling children to find their own pathway to improving and learning the game through golf based challenges that require no technical thought but bags of instinctive feelings. I went to view his coaching once a few years back and stumbled across a great phrase that he told one of the children who found himself in a bunker. 'Try and hit the top layer of sand out onto the grass bank in front of you' he said to this 9 year old budding golfer. And, low and behold, the young golfer dually struck the ball and landed in the middle of the green. How simple but how effective is that? Excited to try that out with my next bunker lesson, I said that exact same thing to a gentleman who had been struggling out of bunkers for years. It was a revelation to him! During his struggles he said he tried every swing fix going to get that ball consistently out of the bunker, from steep shaft and shallow shaft, to open face to closed face, he tried it all. And the diagnosis...... he struck a little bit of sand out onto the grass bank and hey presto! A ball that ends up more often than not on the green.

The best ways are usually the most instinctive ways without concentrating on technique like this drill or focusing on the club's position which we obviously can't see during the swinging action.

However, I see a lot of 'rounded swing' golfers struggle out of bunkers generally. This is a group of golfers who swing the club around their body, enabling the shaft to be near to parallel to the ground on the way back. This is no good for bunker technique as a rounded swing will force the club to reach ground way before the ball or not at all.

Little ball before the big ball

I love this saying, it tells us a lot about where the club should meet the ground in the golf swing…. The low point! A vital component in better ball striking. Too far behind the ball and we get a big splodge of mud. If the low point is not even on the ground, we get that thin shot which sends those horrible vibrations up the club shaft into the hands. Especially unpleasant in the winter time.

There are too many coaches to name here that have given me this phrase but it's popular for a reason. It is simply saying we need to hit the ball (the little ball) before the earth (the big ball)! It's simple genius and so true.

Ensure the club is striking the little ball, then (3 or so inches later) hit the big ball! Simples!!!

Methods

I'm going to be a tad controversial here. A method of teaching (stack and tilt, rotary swing, gravity golf etc) is a way that golf coaches and the founders of these methods market and promote their coaching. Cue numerous lawsuits!

There is no one way of swinging. There can't be. We are all different. There are impact rules, but no one has written a rule book saying 'you must swing the club like this'.......... I stand corrected, there HAS been books written like this, but they must be ignored!!!

These swing methods teach one way of swinging and imply there is one way of swinging the golf club and achieving results which is plain wrong. There are numerous ways of swinging and achieving great results, some orthodox some not so orthodox. We are all different physically, different heights, strengths, weak points, age etc. But ultimately the player who plays the best gets to the point of impact with the ball in the most consistent and efficient way, whatever happens before that to the club or body.

Feel and real

Some years ago, I heard a phrase that was to change the way I teach....... 'Feel and real are two different things'
Play that phrase back through your mind!
In other words, what we feel might not be what we are trying to achieve in our golf swing.
For example, a player who slices the ball might have seen a cure on YouTube where the instructor says, 'attack the ball from the inside'. Enthusiastically, the player gets to the range to try and attack the ball from the inside in desperation mode to ensure the slice is gone forever. But the shots get worse, even

further left to right and missing the middle of the club almost everytime. The player is then very confused. He FEELS the club is coming from the inside (clubhead behind him on the way down) but the shots are worse! The feeling is very different from the real. The real is shown to us in the ball flight. That cannot lie! The ball is told to travel where the club tells it to go. The player might perceive he is performing the correct action, but the flight of the ball tells us that's not quite happening. Frustration then is encountered as the player believed what he saw to cure his slice but has made his golf worse.

This is just one example and it doesn't happen all of the time, but in my experience, this is a fairly common occurrence.

The moral of the story............ don't necessarily think you are producing the swing you need to, look at what the ball flight does first. That will tell you everything!

The Practice Swing

If I had a penny for everyone who has said to me 'Richard, my practice swing is superb, it feels great, but when I get up to the ball and take a swing, it feels completely different', I'd be well on my way to the Seychelles and retiring with a lot of money in the bank!

It's true, more often than not practice swings do feel better than your actual swing. How could this be though if both swings were performed very closely in time to each other? There is a simple explanation to this very common of quandaries............ there is no consequence to the practice swing! If we make a bad practice swing, we don't have the consequence of losing the ball, we don't have the consequence of possibly hitting a bad shot, we're just simply swinging the club with nothing in the way. It's purely based on aesthetics, the way the swing looks and equate it to being a good shot. When we get to the ball however things change. There is a little white ball in front of us that we have to somehow manoeuvre from point A to point B with, more often than not, some hazards in our way. The conscious brain then switches on to try and help us avoid these hazards, we become more 'aware' of the swing and hey presto, we don't feel the swing to be anywhere near as fluid a motion during the actual striking of the ball compared to the practice swing.

In my experience, the best way whenever a golfer has mentioned this to me I have dealt with it is purely to let them feel the fluidity of the practice swing during the course of the golf shot and letting the ball get in the way of the swing, just like we let the ground get in the way of a free-flowing motion of the practice swing.
Don't try and copy your positions in the practice swing, practice the fluidity you feel in it.

<u>Who wants to learn Golf?</u>

It's the great British motto...... why pay money to learn something when you can do it yourself?

I'm sure it's a pride thing, but I have had many a person approach me for lessons and say 'don't tell my friends I've had lessons otherwise they would take the piss out of me', or the classic 'my friends will take the piss if I finish last in our annual golf outing and I'll look like a fool'.

I get the feeling this doesn't happen much in places like America and Europe. The Americans and most Europeans love to learn and take a certain pride in learning as they know they will improve. In Germany for example golfers are required to pass a certification test and take lessons before they are allowed out onto a golf course. Yes, they are actually told to take lessons before they venture out onto a course. Of course there are arguments for and arguments against this procedure, but the fact remains that there is a very different attitude to learning in the UK compared to other countries around the world.
It is one of my goals to help turn around this attitude to learning and learn to embrace it rather than see it as a bad thing.

Yes, self-diagnosis is very satisfying, learning how to do something on your own and do it to an ability you are happy with, but would you honestly re-wire your house if you weren't certified and learnt how to do it on YouTube? So why do golfers do it?

Learn from the best

It has always been my aim to get in contact with as many of the top coaches and top players as I can to pick their brains to help me understand the game of golf better. I hope many golfers out there do the same. Make it your priority if you want to play better golf to learn off the best, whether it be players or whether it be a coach. Like any informative book, get a recommendation. Listen and learn to what they have to say when it comes to the mental side of the game as these better players have been there and experienced it.

Dedication

I remember as a kid, one very snowy winters day, begging my mom and dad to take me up to the golf club as I wanted to practice. There were a good few inches of snow on the ground, but despite trying to talk me out of it, my mom took me to practice for an hour or two. I had a lot of fun, teeing up balls on the snow, seeing how the ball reacted when it hit the frosty green and seeing how close I could get each of the balls to stop close to each other..... easy to see when they plug in the snow.

Now, I don't know whether it's me getting old or not but there seems to be a lack of dedication in a lot of under 18-year-old golfers who have a bundle of talent but like a nice easy life. Therefore, staying indoors when the mercury doesn't get above 5 degrees Celsius. Like anything in life, to be successful, you need hard work which needs dedication. Now I'm not saying that all talented under 18's want to play golf for a living, but even the ones that do lack that dedication and come up with excuses as opposed to reasons they should go out and practice.

With a lot of distractions in modern life such as video games, the internet and a gazillion box sets and TV shows, there is more of a need for that instant gratification as opposed to looking as long term development.

I hope this trend does subside and all players of this great game find a reason to go out and play and not an excuse not to.

Never picked up a club? You're a welcome addition

I love teaching complete beginners. It's a hugely satisfying experience. A fresh start, a blank page. Beginners normally get very nervous when they walk into the teaching bay, not knowing what to expect. I always try and put them at ease first, letting them know they're coming here and playing the game for fun and I'm not trying to test them then laugh at them as they miss their 10th ball in a row.

It is a daunting thing to a lot of people, learning a new game for which there has been so much written about and diving into the unknown puts a lot of people out of their comfort zones. Definitely not a bad thing to be out of your comfort zone every now and again!

I keep things simple. Hold of the club, where the ball has to make contact with the club and let them go for it. Use their instincts and don't teach anyone's instincts out of them.

'The Good Coaches know what to change. The best Coaches know what to leave alone'

The worst thing any coach can do when the beginner leaves a lesson for the first time is have them walking away saying to themselves 'my good god, that was intense and difficult'. The player needs to walk away refreshed, feeling something has been accomplished and want to come back for more. And that is the satisfying part when they feel like that!

Gimmes should be banned

I'm going to cause another round of controversy here. The famous 'gimme'…… a usually short putt in a friendly game of matchplay should be banned! (Cue gasps of discontentment).

For anyone that's looking to get better at the game, I often hear of these players be cursing the short putts as 'card wreckers'. In what seems what of the simplest shots in golf, they miss them a significant percentage of the time and confidence is low.
So how is anyone going to get better at short putts if they are <u>given</u> a significant percentage of the time?

Truth is, it's not going to happen. You can't get better at anything in life if you don't do anything, and practising the short putts is a crucial aspect to the game. The knee wobblers, the tear jerkers, call them what you will, but practise them. Even if it means you get nervous over them and miss the majority, you're still learning about how to deal with them.
If anyone says 'take it away' when you have a 2 footer in front of you tell them 'no thanks, I need to see this one in' and see how much you improve and learn to handle what is a deemed as one of the most simple shots of the game.

Take the breaks, both good and bad

I had a pupil come to me many years ago, a good golfer, complaining that he had too many bad breaks on the golf course and that his constant practice (he didn't practice at much as he believed he did) didn't deserve these bad breaks he was getting.

The truth is that no matter what level of golfer we are, bad breaks are inevitable. The odd bad bounce here and there, the odd bad kick off the tree are all part of this game. I guess that's why some Americans didn't want to play in The Open Championship years ago with its unpredictability and the variation of bounces that you get on what is commonly ground that is baked and hard. It's deemed as 'unfair.'

This is also a rather substantial reason a lot of extremely good golfers and ball strikers struggle to reach their level of potential because they cannot accept the unpredictability that Golf brings. I can see what they mean, all the hard effort they have put in goes unrewarded due to a few unlucky bounces.

Get over it! Golf, like life, isn't always fair. The good luck sometimes feels never ending when things are going our way, we can't put a foot wrong. Then, when we get stuck in a rut, it feels like we have nothing but the bad part of luck we can't get a break! We have to deal with it and learn to accept it. It is a part of who we are and in general, bad things happen even if we don't deserve them. In my experience, again in golf as in life, the successful ones overcome the bad breaks a lot quicker than the least successful.

Bad luck happens, whether we play off a 36 handicap or are an elite playing professional. Get over it, laugh it off, do what you can to forget it and you will not only become a better player, you will also become a happier person.

Europe v USA – The one-sided cup

I hope my American friends don't get too upset with me here. It seems that Europe have been winning most of the biennial contests this past couple of decades and it's interesting trying to find out why this is the case.

It was for so many years a one-sided contest in the favour of the Americans. For what seemed like an eternity since the Ryder Cups birth in 1927, the players from the west side of the Atlantic Ocean came out on top. Well they did have some of the greatest golfers to ever play the game which helped a lot.

Now it seems that Europe are the dominant force. At time of of publication, from 1985 up until the contest of 2016, Europe have won 10 matches, the USA 5 matches and one tied. A fair reflection of Europe's dominance.

But why has this been such a dominant time for Europe?
There have been many ideas floating around from various insiders, journalists, coaches and everyone associated with the game as the Ryder Cup is seen as the pinnacle for a lot of players. To participate in the matches is seen as the crème de la crème of the game. The reason is certainly not to do with either side having an outstanding asset to their team (see Tiger Wood's Ryder Cup record at his peak playing days) so both sets of players are set up very evenly. The explanation is simple...... teamwork! The European team have bonded exceptionally well and have supported each other, celebrated with each other and picked one another up when not playing to their ability. It seems the Americans have not succeeded in doing this very well during the past 3 decades, therefore they have paid the penalty, especially when some of the matches have not been that close at all.
I have a feeling that from now on, the Americans will come back with a vengeance. Just watch this space.

<u>Golf is great because...........</u>

- We play on varied land
- We can play the courses the pros play

- We can play with our friends
- We can beat our enemies
- We can relax
- We can speed up
- We can play competitively
- We can play socially
- We can play in other countries
- We can do business whilst playing
- We exercise
- We can play at almost any age

Just a few of the reasons I believe we are all fortunate to be involved with the world's greatest game

I swing too fast!!!

No you don't. Period! It is remarkable how many golfers, high handicappers mainly, who think they swing the club too fast. Don't get me wrong, I understand why they think like this. Whenever they play poorly, the club and the body feel like they move independently, the swing doesn't feel in sync and the shots tend to be inaccurate with poor contact. The golfers brain, because it is feeling the motion, is telling the player he is swinging too fast and that is the reason the shots are poor.

It makes sense in some ways. We are out of sync so we try and swing slower to be more in sync. Right??? WRONG!!!

The more we slow our swing down, the less chance we have of making good contact with the ball. Why? Because we are stopping the momentum of the golf swing (see previous story on 'DON'T PUT THE BRAKES ON') which in turn can put the club into the wrong positions. I know this goes a little against the grain as to what someone has told you but trust me, I have seen a lot more golfers struggle with a purposeful slower swing compared to those with a swing where they actually HIT the ball, not trying to control the club to the ball.

Golf live

Go and watch the pros live and close up. Wherever you can. A PGA Tour event, a European Tour event, even one of the mini tour events such as The Europro Tour. It is a great experience to see what some of the best players out there are doing, how they strike the ball and how they think and get round the golf course in the least amount of shots, even when they aren't playing very well.

But go on one of the practice days, usually a Tuesday if you can sneak off work early or you work for yourself. You can get far closer to the players then with no crowds around and some even allow cameras on the practice days.

I remember going to my first event my dad took me to. It was the English Open at The Belfry and it was my first real introduction to how the best in the world played the game. To follow the likes of Monty, Seve, Howard Clarke and Barry Lane at that period was like gold dust to me. It spurred me on to think that these guys can achieve this and are playing at a top venue like this, why can't I achieve this?

The flight and sound of the ball being struck stood out for me more than anything. I didn't really watch the swings, I just listened to the sound of the ball being hit and the endless flight it seemed to take. It was a joy to watch and made me go back to my local course and just hit balls to see if I can replicate what they did. It gave a huge sense of motivation to try and achieve the life of the pro and the things they could do with the golf ball.

Card in your hand

Going into a tournament or a monthly medal or stableford or any game where you have a card in your hand. Yes, that little piece of recycled (mostly) card that you write down your scores on, whether they are low scores or high scores.

Many golfers take a different approach to preparing for a game that bears even some slight significance to them like a monthly medal or regional event where scores are of the essence.

Through all the play and practice that golfers often do, ensuring their game is in tip top condition for the following weeks medal, a chance to beat handicap and get cut, a chance to win prizes, whether it be silverware or a small amount of money to spend in the pro shop. All that hard practice could go to waste however. I often ask, when people have a great run up to an event in regard to play and practice, but perform poorly during the course of play, about what they did the night before! Now I'm not prying into their private life, just purely to see if there something different about it as all signs led to a good one. And, looking into golfers habits the night before a friendly game and the prep done the night before in the medal, it's just you and the course. So what happens?

We start changing our habits the night before as we think, to get the most out of our game, we need to change our habits. For example, if you usually go to the pub on Friday night with your mates but this time you've called it off as youre playing golf then you're doing the wrong thing. Your prep should mirror anything close to what you would usually do. Going to bed 2 hours earlier, not going to the pub if you usually would are both not good if theyre out of routine. You will have a much better chance if you go through your normal routine. Why? Because if you steer away from normal routine in the day before a medal, chances are you will be feeling like you're helping yourself. Not the case! Having an early night or not going to your usual pub routine with your mates can show to yourself you are placing too much significance on the game of golf when it's just that, it's a game, whether you shoot a course record or 20 strokes above handicap.

<u>Remember your good shots</u>

If you only take one thing away from this book this should be it. We all have the ability to hit great golf shots...... yes, the pros a few more good shots than any mid to high handicapper, but it's incredible to hear players who describe their games whenever I ask them about it.

Phrases such as 'I lost so many golf balls' or 'I took 4 shots to get out of this one trap' or 'I 3 putted umpteen times' are rife and are usually first to be mentioned when talking about their previous round of golf. As adults, we almost expect things to go wrong. We are less disappointed then because it meets our negative expectations. We don't want to set the bar too high as we are then hugely disappointed if we don't meet those high levels of achievement. So we therefore expect to fail, we expect to hit bad shots. Never a great thought when approaching the round of golf, standing on the first tee saying to ourselves 'I hate this shot, I hit it way right here last time I played it'.

I can almost bet you're reading this and thinking 'I'm never going to do that, I don't hit any good shots and it's too much work'. Trust me, you will be a better golfer if you do write down and place your best shots under the limelight. It only has to be one or two shots but make it a habit.

Sternum control

The sternum (the breastbone) is an integral part in the golf swing and I regularly mention this in instruction. The position of the sternum is a big (but not the only) reason the club either catches the ground before, after, or on top of the ball. Imagine a line from the sternum down to the ground or even place your club on your sternum at your address position and see where it is in relation to the ball. If your sternum is behind the ball at impact, you will more than likely catch the ground before the ball. If the sternum is in front of the ball at impact, you will more than likely enable the club to catch the ground in front of the ball which is necessary for your irons. Indeed, the position of the sternum at impact can different from that of address, but checking it at address will help make you aware of what it's like at impact and the feeling you need. With the driver, the sternum slightly behind the ball is advisable to encourage a slightly upward angle of attack. With the irons, slightly in front of the ball at impact is advisable to encourage a slightly downward angle of attack.

Helping the club achieve the correct 'low point' to the ground is crucial in helping you contact the ball as efficiently as possible. No one enjoys having a big splodge of mud flying into your face when you take a shot!!!

Check your sternum position at address, you might be surprised.

__Too many wedges spoil the broth__

I am very much an advocate of golfers, no matter what level you are at, copying something one of the top players does, whether it be what they think on the course, what a certain swing thought is and so on. However, I think amateurs (high handicappers in particular) would do best to stay well away from this one………. Putting more than 3 wedges in the bag! With the expertise the pros show in their short game, the finesse, the touch, it's brilliant to watch. I notice a lot of amateurs, in need of a better short game and touch around the green, investing in numerous wedges with lofts no more than 4 degrees apart starting from a modern day 45-degree Pitching Wedge, all the way through to a 60 degree lob wedge. I always advise someone who has a weak chipping and pitching action never to invest in a lob wedge!

'Why' I hear you cry.

To put simply, to be a great chipper and pitcher of the ball, you need to have the ability to 'control the loft and bounce on the club'. For example, if you have a wedge which says 52 degrees on it, to control the trajectory of the shot (the flight path) and contact the ball as well as you possibly can, you need to have the ability to 'feel' what the loft is at impact. This is controlled by either leaning the handle of the club towards the target or slightly away from the target.

Now, when a high handicapper hits a chip or a pitch, the likely outcome is he/she will thin it through the green or duff it barely 3 yards in front of them. Why is this? In my experience most golfers try and lift or scoop the ball up in the air, trying to, subconsciously, add loft to the golf club. This doesn't make sense however since there is already a lot of loft on the club itself...... in this case 52 degrees! The results are even more disastrous with a lob wedge. If we catch the ball well and we increase the loft at the same time, guess what's going to happen? The ball flies up the air barely reaching half way to your target. Next time when we swing the lob wedge? We put a longer swing on it as we are reacting to the result we got previously. The danger in this is if we don't catch the ball very well we run a massive risk of thinning it and, combined with a long and powerful swing, is a recipe for that ball shooting 50-80 yards past the green......... a highly embarrassing result!

One of the keys to good golf as mentioned previously is to keep things simple. Investing in 4 wedges is giving the golfer far too much choice over the shot which leads to confusion which leads to poor short game play. Learn how to play a variety of shots with one club.

Do yourself a favour........ stick to 3 wedges maximum (pitching wedge, gap wedge and sand wedge) and learn how to manufacture shots with them, hit it high, hit it low, but most of all, get to know them and love them before discarding them for a lob wedge and confusin your short game even more.

Perfect my Golf.....or not!!!!

Quite simply, as golf is full of variations, clubs, distances, environment, weather, ground conditions, player feel and more, there is NO chance of anyone playing perfect golf. It just doesn't exist.

Now baking a cake, that's different. You can perfect that. You are in control of the temperature of the oven, you are in control of the ingredients and their values, you can bake the perfect cake.

Golf is just not a game of perfect!

The 80-20 rule

Why do so many high handicap golfers struggle with pitching and chipping? It seems like a simple shot. Picture the scene........... 400 yard par 4, Joe Handicap is off 27. Joe, who has never been a long hitter of the ball, gets to within 50 yards of the green in 2 shots. He's chuffed to bits! Never in his life has he got this close to a hole of this length before. But wait!!!

Thoughts enter Joes head such as 'oh no, I hope I don't mess this hole up now ive done the hard work to get here' or 'I can't remember how far I've got to swing the club back and through on a 50 yard shot'. Joe, with these thoughts in his mind, gets up to the shot, starts shaking and sweating over it and…………oh dear…………… thins it through the green. On his next shot, as a reaction to the previous shot, duffs it 3 feet in front of him. Now he's not on the green for 4 shots after being close in 2! How frustrating……. But how common!!!

A lot of this was very much down to Joe's thought process. He was thinking about the length of the swing he had to take and not about visualising the shot he had to play, merely not wanting to mess things up after he felt he did the hard work to come as close to the green as he ever has.

There is a simple rule I help golfers who don't practice their pitching or chipping and it's the 80-20 rule…… the ball travels 80% in the air and rolls another 20%. I see a lot of players try and fly the ball to the hole. Well that's great but your chances of directly flying the ball into the hole is extremely small. You have to allow for the roll of the ball as it comes into the green. It can't just pitch and stop (despite what you might see on the TV). The average golfer hasn't got the equipment and the conditions and skill level to produce a shot that runs in low, checks twice and then comes to a grinding halt. A hugely attractive shot and one that woo's the crowds, but unrealistic to play for the majority of golfers.

Play for the 80-20 rule.

'I wannabe consistent'

It's a phrase that's used almost as much as 'keep your head down'. Excluding beginners, the majority of golfers has their goal set to be more consistent. Continuity in life is usually a good thing. Something we can predict, no surprises and very few disappointments. The same goes for golf, the ability to swing the club the same, the ability to hit the ball in the designated target every single time, the ability to predict every outcome of every shot every single time. Is this possible?
In a word............NO!

With the variable nature of the game of golf, the environment, different types courses, different clubs used for different shots, different arenas where golf is played such as driving range or course, it is impossible to be able to hit every single shot the way you intended. A 6 iron speed is approximately 70mph (for an 18 handicap on average), the clubhead travels approximately 6 metres during the swing, the golf ball is 1.68 inches in diameter, the sweet spot on the golf club face is about the size of a finger nail. As you can see all these factors are difficult to get absolutely spot on with every shot you take. Add the environment factors in, the pressure of competition and a few swing thoughts and you realise that consistency in golf is non-existent. Not even Iron

Byron, the famous swinging robot, can swing the club exactly the same all the time.
So don't try and be consistent. It's impossible. Look to get better and accept even small improvements, whether that be in your scores, striking ability or short game and don't give yourself a hard time if you screw up or shoot a worse score than you did last week. It's inevitable in this game and that's what keeps us coming back for more.

<u>Grip Pressure</u>

I conducted a survey of a number of golf pros several years ago as this was a question I didn't have an answer to. How firm do we have to hold the club?

I'd heard such stories such as 'holding a baby chick' or 'squeezing toothpaste from a tube'.

Then one pro, who also researched the answer to this question, came up with the golden nugget I was looking for………. FIRM IN THE FINGERS BUT LOOSE IN THE WRISTS!

A 6 out of 10 if you were on the grip pressure scale. We have to hold the club firm as it's travelling at a fair rate of knots during the swing, but we have to allow the wrists to work during the action and they would be unable to if we shut them off through being too stiff.

Keep hold of the club, but not to the detriment of the wrists!

No Excuses

Because golf is an individual game, mistakes that a player makes stand out, as they are the only ones accountable for their actions and score. Football, for example, has 11 men per side and if you have a stinker of a game but the team still wins you can be let off the hook with poor performance. Granted, in this day and age with cameras on every player in the premier league, that stinker of a game might not go unnoticed but in most football that is played it isn't necessarily like that.

It seems to be rife in younger players who wish to play professionally on the tours. Every bad round they play makes them feel inadequate and therefore the excuses come out........... 'the weather was dreadful' (even though it might have been the same for everyone), 'didn't like the course/course was poor' (again, same for everyone), 'I had the wrong glove on' and I have even heard the classic 'my fingernails were too long'....... This is absolutely genuine!

As you can see, plenty of excuses, which may be all true and valid reasons as to poor performance. But how does the upcoming professional learn from inevitable performances that don't live up to their expectations? Truth is they don't. No one can learn from excuses, we only learn from admitting our mistakes. There must be reasons for a below average score or performance that can be practised and improved upon, whether it be a swing fault or not quite the right mindset going into your shots.

Stress? On the course?

Isn't golf meant to be your leisure time?
Our time is very precious to us in this modern-day world. Distractions are ever present as we seek to do what's best but get caught up when something we find more fun comes our way.
Golf can be very stressful to a lot of people. The anticipation of that weekend game after a long and difficult week at work can seem like the perfect retreat from the everyday problems faced in the workplace.
The calm and tranquil nature of the game can be just the tonic that the working adult needs to help them de-stress.
The anticipation is rife. They go to the course with great prospects and start the day on a huge high.

However, bad shots start to creep in, the odd hook, the odd shank in there. The brain and body start to get angry and tense. And it's only the 4th hole!!! We then try everything in our power to put it right as we cannot continue in our mind to hit it like this otherwise embarrassment and the possibility of unsavoury banter from our regular playing partners starts to plague us. Every swing tip we have ever heard creeps into our mind and makes things worse due to the complete 'paralysis by analysis'. The game continues to get worse and by the 9th hole we just want to walk in, sinking our sorrows in the club's guest ale.

But what happened? We started so confidently and our anticipation for a great day's golf was high. So why on earth did we self-destruct?

The answer? Our 'chimp' got hold of our thinking! According to Dr Steven Peters, our mind is made up of the chimp, the human and the computer. The human is the rational thinker, the chimp controls the emotions and the computer puts these two together. When we hit a few bad shots on the course, we tend to react negatively, whether that means frustration or anger. Our chimp takes over with irrational thoughts. 'Why am I so bad at this game'? 'This happened last week, why don't I learn from these mistakes'? These are just a couple of questions we ask ourselves. But the real question is, do these help us to get better?

Categorically and without a shadow of a doubt........no!

It's because the irrational chimp has taken over and disrupted our original happy human flow of mind and seen bad shots as food to feed its negativity.

The answer to stop this awful feeling on the course? Quieten the chimp. Recognise it is there and recognise it's completely irrational in the way it is delivering its message to us. Let the sensible human run the show and learn that bad shots do occur whatever level of golfer you are, it's one of those things. It's how we deal with it on course is what makes us drive home from the golf course happy or whether we drive home angry with a sense of wasted time. Try not to be the latter.

<u>Left Heel Up</u>

It's fascinating teaching the game of golf with a high-speed video camera. I especially like the moments when a golfer sees their swing for the first time and impressions they have of it.

I tend to hear a few things. 'Wow, didn't realise I took the club back so far'.'Oh, I don't lift my head up'. 'It looks better than I thought'.
One of my personal favourites is this though, 'I shouldn't be lifting my left heel up like that on the way back' (assuming right handed golfer here).
If only golfers watched footage of golf pros and the way they do things as opposed to watching endless footage of the 'how to' way of swinging the club. They would see this occurred a lot, mainly with the older generation of elite golfers such as Nicklaus.

I honestly cannot give a reason as to why people think it's a bad thing. Maybe it's one of those 'tips' that has grown on the grapevine and gone viral into the minds of golfers.
Either way, lifting the left heel is not a bad thing. And let me tell you why. It helps you turn! Turn your hips

and turn your shoulders. And with golf being a predominantly rotary sport, a hip and shoulder turn can all but help you.

Maybe unless you have the flexibility of Inspector Gadget should the heel be kept on the floor, but let's face it, who has got that flexibility?

Be Humble

I recently heard a story of a journalist who had planned and played his very last round of Golf due to a debilitating illness that was making him physically weaker each passing day. He knew he would be unable to play again.

Put yourself in his shoes, knowing that tomorrow you might be playing your very last round of Golf.

Make it count. Make every day count.

If you like this, please subscribe to my blog at
www.richardcartwrightgolf.co.uk

Contact me direct at
richardcartwrightgolf@gmail.com for any feedback.

With thanks to Whittlebury Park for all your support.
Truly grateful to be a part of one of the UK's finest
facilities.

Printed in Poland
by Amazon Fulfillment
Poland Sp. z o.o., Wrocław